IN

FOR

BRITISH
SERVICEMEN
IN
GERMANY
1944

ISBN 978 1 85124 351 8

First published by the Foreign Office, 1943
Introduction and this edition © Bodleian Library, University of Oxford, 2007
Broad Street, Oxford OX1 3BG
www.bodleianshop.co.uk

This edition first published in 2007
Reprinted 2007, 2008, 2011, 2014, 2016, 2019
All rights reserved

Designed by Dot Little
Typeset by JCS Publishing Services, www.jcs-publishing.co.uk in Gill Sans 8/13.5
Printed and bound in China by C&C Offset Printing Co. Ltd
on 100gsm Chinese Sen Lawrence woodfree

British Library Cataloguing in Publication Data
A CIP record of this publication is available from the British Library

CONTENTS

EDITOR'S NOTE

The 'Words and Phrases' section is printed in abridged form.

PREFACE

Nine and a half months after D-Day, thirty thousand British troops crossed the Rhine as part of the Allied assault on Germany. As early as May 1943 suggestions had been made that the troops should be issued with some kind of written guidance as to how they should counter the views of Germans they might come into contact with as part of an army of occupation, and, after considerable discussion, this pamphlet was the result.

Like the earlier *Instructions to British Servicemen in France* (also republished by the Bodleian Library) the aim was to educate the soldiers on a range of topics, including German history, the national character, politics, culture, food, drink, currency and language, as well as to explain the current situation, including the effect of the war on Germany and German attitudes to the British. There was, however, one crucial difference. Whereas the underlying aim of the earlier booklet had been to bring together two allies who, although they had not always had the easiest of relationships during the war, had many common objectives and values, the principal aim this time was to condition the troops against the effects of German propaganda, and to restrict the contacts between the occupiers and the occupied to the minimum.

Those who drew it up were painfully aware that an earlier British army of occupation in Germany after the First World War had failed to destroy what they perceived as the overwhelming tendencies in German history towards militarism and conquest. They were also aware of the hold Nazi propaganda had over the German population, and were determined that the British troops should know how to counter it. This led them to three principal conclusions: that all Germans, whether members of the Nazi Party or not, should be held responsible for the war, that the Germans had 'much to unlearn', and that there should be no fraternisation between the occupiers and the occupied. As the booklet states, their view was that 'There will be no brutality about a British occupation, but neither will there be softness or sentimentality'. This line was echoed by Field Marshal Montgomery in his message to the troops, where he said; 'The defeated enemy must be made to put his house in order ... Also he must be made to pay for the war which was of his making ... We shall try to be wise as conquerors. As we were strong in battle, so we shall be just in peace.' It is thus apparent from the start that the tone of this booklet is markedly different from the earlier ones published in this series. Those were produced to introduce Allied soldiers to friendly countries, and although they were serious in intent, they were also quite light-hearted in tone. There is little that was intended to be light-hearted in the text presented here.

The general tone of the booklet is stated at its most stark in the Security Note at the end: 'Germans must still be regarded as dangerous enemies until the final Peace Settlement has been concluded and after the occupation of Germany has ended'. Much of the text was therefore devoted to warning soldiers against feeling sorry for the Germans. This theme appears in the very first paragraph of the foreword:

> You will see much suffering in Germany and much to awake your pity. You may also find that many Germans, on the surface at least, seem pleasant enough and that they will even try to welcome you as friends.
>
> All this may make you think they have learned their lesson and need no further teaching. But remember this ... [t]he Germans have much to unlearn.
>
> They also have much to atone for.

The booklet then goes on the state that 'The German people as a whole cannot escape a large share of responsibility', and that even the plot against Hitler was not a revolt against 'the barbarity of Hitler's methods, but merely their lack of success'. Fraternisation between the British troops and German civilians was at first forbidden by the Allied High Command, although, as the booklet says, 'there will probably be occasions when you will have to deal with them, and for that reason it is necessary to know something about what sort of people they are'. Later the rules were relaxed somewhat, at first permitting conversations in the street, but later allowing a much greater degree of social contact, although even then the troops were officially forbidden to marry German women.

It is interesting to compare this booklet with a training film called *Your Job in Germany*, which was issued at around the same time. It was made by the U.S. Army but was also shown to British and other Allied troops about to enter Germany. If anything it takes an even harder line towards the German population, whether they were civilians or not. There is, for example, a similar emphasis on German history. At one point the commentary says: 'You'll see some mighty pretty scenery. Don't let it fool you. You are in enemy country. Be alert, suspicious of everyone. Take no chances. You are up against more than tourist scenery. You are up against German history. It isn't good.'

The film refers to German aggression in 1870, 1914 and 1939, and then states: 'The German lust for conquest is not dead. It's merely gone under cover . . . It can happen again. That is why you occupy Germany, to make that next war impossible'. And the troops were again warned against fraternisation, the film telling them that 'Fraternisation means making friends. The German people are not our friends. You will not associate with German men, women or children.' For a time around December 1944 Allied soldiers could even be fined the not inconsiderable sum of £16 for fraternising with the enemy.

Over sixty years later, and after a long period of peace in Europe during which Germany and Britain have been allies and partners in NATO and the European Union, these exhortations read decidedly oddly, and one might think that there was far more to be gained in the long run by encouraging fraternisation between the troops and the German civilian population, than by warning against it. And there is, in fact, some evidence that many of Britain's civilian and military leaders were unhappy with it at the time. Churchill's famous epigraph at the end of his *History of the Second World War*—'In war, resolution; in defeat, defiance; in victory, magnanimity; in peace, good will'—suggests that he had a broader and more humane vision of the future than the writers of the *Instructions*; and Field Marshal Montgomery, despite the firm line in his message to the troops in September 1945, later wrote in his memoirs that 'if ever we were to re-educate the German population it would be a good thing to mix freely with them and teach them our standards of freedom and individual responsibility'.

As for the views of the rank-and-file British soldiers, these were neatly expressed in a cartoon by Giles in the *Daily Express*, published on 22 July 1945. This shows a crowd of German women pursuing two British soldiers through a wood, whilst two other girls hold a trip wire across the path in front of them. The caption reads 'Rough on us chaps that don't want to fraternise, isn't it?'.

The troops were also able to express their views of Germany and the Germans through the letters columns of the *British Zone Review*, a fortnightly newspaper produced by the Information Services Division of the Control Commission for Germany between 1945 and 1949. As early as the second issue, there was a letter expressing pity for at least some of the population. Lucia Lawson, a subaltern in the A.T.S., wrote:

It is hard to believe when we have just come through six years of a war which was not of our making that anyone can feel sorry for the people who caused it, but I challenge any average man or woman to spend one week in Berlin and not feel some small measure of pity for some Berliners.

This letter generated quite a lot of correspondence in the *British Zone Review*, as well as an editorial which stated unequivocaly that 'first and foremost we must be firm'. The troops themselves expressed a wide variety of opinions. It has to be said that the clear majority were in favour of the official line. Sergeant R.J. Dolamore, for example, wrote that:

We all want to avoid another war in the future and to do this the only way is to teach the Germans that war does not pay. We shall never do this by feeling sorry for them. Let them suffer all the hardships possible for the next 10 years, and probably by that time the lesson will have entered their thick heads.

This line was fairly common. Sergeant J.P. Noonan, on the other hand, thought that a more liberal approach would be more productive:

We have called ourselves the Army of Liberation, the Crusaders of Truth, Justice and Liberty. If we are democrats and liberators of the oppressed, entrusted with the mission of enlightening and teaching the principles of truth, justice and liberty, then in the name of logic and commonsense, why not practice what we preach? Humanity and justice cannot be based upon hatred and revenge. Our mission is to show the Germans that they failed because they ignored all principles of humanity. We must punish the criminals responsible and teach the others by example that we have something better to offer.

A similar view was put forward by someone who signed himself 'D.G., Hannover':

> I would suggest three rules ... First, that merely because the Germans have been wicked, we are not justified in a similar retributive offence. It is nearly two thousand years since a better formula than an eye for an eye was suggested. Our standards must be our own, and be kinder than those of the National Socialists, or I do not know for what positive aim we fought.
>
> The second rule is that one should be kind where one is. These wise men who say never be kind to Germans, reserve your sympathy for the French, Yugoslavs or Greeks, speak a half-truth. Of course one is sympathetic towards such innocent victims of German aggression ... But ... sooner than see kindness in the wrong place, some people would see no kindness at all.
>
> The last rule which occurs to one is that one should remember that Western Europe is a cultural entity ... Germany is ... a major contributor to the civilization of Western Europe, and one whose destruction will impoverish us all.

And a Dutch interpreter added this thought: 'Surely it would be better to concentrate on telling the people what is right ... Forget the past, abolish recriminations, remember that the Germans are thinkers, that they too have brains and pride.'

In the long run, it was this more generous view that was to prevail, helped to a considerable degree by the onset of the Cold War, which led to a major shift in the official view, from treating Germany as a defeated enemy to building her up as a potential ally against the new Soviet threat. Gradually a blind eye was turned to people's Nazi pasts, and the official policy on all sides became what Konrad Adenauer called in his first address to the parliament of the newly constituted Federal Republic of Germany on 20 September 1949, the determination 'to put the past behind us'. This 'collective amnesia', it has been argued, undoubtedly benefited Europe during the post-war period.[1]

Dating from the pre-Cold War period, this pamphlet retains its interest as a snapshot of the official view at a time when Germany rather than the Soviet Union was seen as the greatest threat to future peace in Europe. However, it also reflects much more widely held views of German history and culture and the character of the German people, which, in Britain, can be dated back to the last quarter of the nineteenth century, following German unification after the Franco-Prussian war of 1870–71. In turn unintentionally humorous and crudely stereotypical, it thus reveals as much about British wartime attitudes and prejudices as it does of the devastated Germany the Allied soldiers were about to encounter for the first time.

John Pinfold
Bodleian Library

1   T. Judt, *Postwar: A History of Europe Since 1945* (London, 2005), pp. 61–2.

INSTRUCTIONS

FOR

BRITISH SERVICEMEN

IN

GERMANY

Prepared by
The Political Warfare Executive

Issued by
The Foreign Office,
London

1944

This book has nothing to do with military operations.

It deals only with civilian life in Germany and with the way you should behave to the German civilian population.

This book is published in November, 1944, at a time when our Armies have barely entered Germany and Hitler and the Nazi regime have not yet been overthrown. Many important events may happen between now and the time when you first read this book. Do not be surprised therefore if here and there sentences, true at the time they were written, have become out of date.

FOR the second time in under thirty years, British troops are entering upon the soil of Germany. The German Army, the most carefully constructed military machine which the world has known, has suffered catastrophic defeats in the field. The civilian population of Germany has seen the war brought into its homes in a terrible form. You will see much suffering in Germany and much to awake your pity. You may also find that many Germans, on the surface at least, seem pleasant enough and that they will even try to welcome you as friends.

All this may make you think that they have learned their lesson and need no further teaching. But remember this: for the last hundred years—long before Hitler—German writers of great authority have been steadily teaching the necessity for war and glorifying it for its own sake. The Germans have much to unlearn.

They have also much to atone for. Never has murder been organised on so vast a scale as by the German Government and the German Army in this war. Death by shooting, hanging, burning, torture or starvation has been visited on hundreds of thousands of civilians in the countries of Eastern Europe occupied by the Germans, and on thousands in the occupied countries of Western Europe.

The record of these outrages is not just "atrocity propaganda." It is based in most cases on the evidence of eye-witnesses or on statements made by the criminals themselves. Moreover, the writings and speeches of the German leaders show that such outrages formed part of a deliberate policy.

The German people as a whole cannot escape a large share of responsibility. The main instruments of German policy were certainly Hitler's Black Guards and Secret Police, but ordinary German officers, N.C.O.'s and men acted often enough with the same brutality. Individual German soldiers and civilians may have deplored it, but no one was found to protest publicly and in good time against it. From the time Hitler came to power no serious resistance movement showed itself in Germany until the attempted putsch of the German generals on the 20th July, 1944. But the cause of that revolt was not the barbarity of Hitler's methods, but merely their lack of success.

The history of these last years must not be repeated. The purpose of the British Commonwealth and its Allies, and of the forces which represent them, is not vengeance against the Germans. It is to make sure that they will never again have the chance to submerge Europe and the world in blood. Remember for as long as you are in Germany that you would not be there at all if German crimes had not made this war inevitable, and that it is only by the sacrifice of thousands upon thousands of your fellow countrymen and Allies, and at a cost of untold suffering at home and abroad through five long years, that British troops are at last on German soil. Think first of all this when you are tempted to sympathise with those who to-day are reaping the fruits of their policy, both in peace and war.

—TO BEGIN WITH—

YOU are going into Germany.

You are going there as part of the Forces of the United Nations which have already dealt shattering blows on many fronts to the German war-machine, the most ruthless the world has ever known.

You will find yourselves, perhaps for some time, among the people of an enemy country; a country that has done its utmost to destroy us—by bombing, by U-boat attacks, by military action whenever its armies could get to grips with ours, and by propaganda.

But most of the people you will see when you get to Germany will not be airmen or soldiers or U-boat crews, but ordinary civilians—men, women and children. Many of them will have suffered from overwork, underfeeding and the effects of air raids, and you may be tempted to feel sorry for them.

You have heard how the German armies behaved in the countries they occupied, most of them neutral countries, attacked without excuse or warning. You have heard how they carried off men and women to forced labour, how they looted, imprisoned, tortured and killed. **There will be no brutality about a British occupation, but neither will there be softness or sentimentality.**

You may see many pitiful sights. Hard-luck stories may somehow reach you. Some of them may be true, at least in part, but most will be hypocritical attempts to win sympathy. For, taken as a whole, the German is brutal when he is winning, and is sorry for himself and whines for sympathy when he is beaten.

So be on your guard against "propaganda" in the form of hard-luck stories. Be fair and just, but don't be soft.

You must also remember that most Germans have heard only the German side of the war and of the events that led up to it. They were forbidden to listen to any news except that put out by their own Propaganda Ministry, and were savagely punished if they disobeyed. So most of them have a completely false impression of what has happened, and will put about—perhaps in good faith—stories that are quite untrue.

The impression you have gained of world events is much nearer the truth than the distorted conceptions spread by the German Propaganda Ministry. So don't let yourself be taken in by plausible statements.

Of course there are Germans who have been against the Nazis all along, though few of those who tried to do anything about it have survived to tell the tale. Even those Germans who have been more or less anti-Nazi will have their axe to grind. But there is no need for you to bother about German attempts to justify themselves. All that matters at present is that you are about to meet a **strange people in a strange, enemy country.**

Your Supreme Commander has issued an order forbidding fraternisation with Germans, but there will probably be occasions when you will have to deal with them, and for that reason it is necessary to know something about what sort of people they are.

GERMANY is a big country.

In area it is twice as big, and in population about one and a half times as big, as England, Scotland, Wales and Northern Ireland together.

As the map on pages 26 and 27 shows you, Germany is landlocked except for the tideless Baltic in the north and a short coastline on the North Sea. In the east and west its frontiers are not defined by great mountains and rivers, which is one reason perhaps why the Germans are always trying to push them further out.

Its greatest rivers, the Rhine, Elbe, Oder and Danube, are not purely German, since they flow through other countries before reaching the sea.

The climate in North-Western Germany is rather like that in Britain, but as you go south or east you will find it hotter in summer and colder in winter than it is at home. There is more rain in Western Germany than in the east, but everywhere you will get more fine, hot days in summer and more crisp, bright cold in winter.

Germany has a great variety of scenery. In the north is a great plain, bare except for occasional pine forests and studded with lakes; it is a continuation of the plains of Russia and Poland. In Central Germany the hilly up-lands are thickly forested. The valley of the Rhine with its sudden hills, its vineyards and old castles, is well known to English tourists, and further south you come through the foothills to the German Alps.

Industry. Germany is highly industrial. The German "Black Country" is in the west on the Rhine and Ruhr, where what is left of the towns of Cologne, Dortmund, Düsseldorf, Duisburg, Essen, Bochum and many others familiar from our Air Ministry reports, form one great continuous industrial area. Other great centres of manufacture are in Thuringia and Saxony (Central Germany) and in the eastern province of Silesia.

The north-western port of Hamburg, which is about half as big again as Glasgow is probably the most "English" of German towns. It has always had close commercial ties with this country.

Seventy years ago, Berlin, the capital, was about the size of Manchester. Now, with a population of nearly four and a half millions, it is over one-third as big as Greater London. It is the seat of government of the German "Reich" and is practically surrounded by a broad belt of industrial plants.

The German transport system was one of the best in Europe. Apart from its excellent railways, much use was made of the great natural waterways, like the Rhine, which were connected by a system of canals. One of

Hitler's positive achievements was to build hundreds of miles of first-class motor-roads, though his object in doing so was largely military. These are called Auto-bahnen (car-ways).

THE most interesting fact about German history is that **Germany did not exist as a nation until 1871**. Before then it consisted of a number of states each with its own court, its own laws and customs barriers. Much the largest of these states was Prussia.

The credit (if one can use the word) for uniting these various kingdoms and grand duchies belongs to a Prussian statesman, **Bismarck**.

Between 1864 and 1871 he engineered three aggressive but successful wars against Denmark, Austria and France, and these victories so impressed the other German States that they entered a confederation under Prussian leadership. This confederation was called the German Reich, and the King of Prussia became German Kaiser (Emperor).

The vices of militarism and aggressiveness, often thought to be peculiar to the Prussians, soon infected the whole of Germany. The Germans acquired colonies, chiefly in Africa; they challenged British sea-power by building a powerful fleet. And in 1914 they thought they were strong enough to enforce an unchallenged supremacy in Europe. In alliance with Austria-Hungary, Turkey and Bulgaria they fought and lost the First World War.

After the defeat of 1918 Germany went through a sort of revolution. This revolution was largely lath and plaster, but was accepted by the Germans because they are used to political shams. Some of the politicians of the German Republic, who succeeded the Kaiser in 1918, meant well: they established a parliamentary system which gave to the ordinary German more individual freedom from then to 1933 than before or since. But behind the scenes the real power still remained in the hands of the generals, the great industrialists and landowners and the professional civil servants. They waited and watched for a chance to assert themselves.

The chance came with the rise of Adolf Hitler.

Rise of Hitler. This ex-corporal of the First Great War was not even a German, but an Austrian who had fought in a German regiment. At first he was considered rather a joke, but his party, the National Socialist German Workers' Party (Nazi for short), gained millions of supporters during the great slump of 1930–32. He promised the workers a form of socialism; he promised the industrialists more power and bigger profits; he promised both that he would wipe out the Versailles Treaty and create a single "Great German" State. The Nationalist Party (Junkers—that is, feudal landowners—generals and industrialists) believed they could use the Nazis to restore their old privileges. So they persuaded the President, Field Marshal von Hindenburg, to make Hitler Chancellor of the Reich. This was in January, 1933.

To secure his election in March, Hitler engineered the Reichstag fire and by attributing it to the Communists made it the excuse for a reign of terror. But the elections in March did not give Hitler's party a clear majority, in spite of the flood of propaganda let loose in his favour from platform, press and radio; the Nationalists, however, supported him, and to make doubly sure he arrested various members of opposition parties who might have voted against him.

His next act was to pass a bill which ended parliamentary government and made him Dictator of Germany.

Then he began to "discipline" the country. Law was suspended. Jews, Communists, Socialists, Liberals—anyone who had publicly opposed him—were hunted down by Hitler's private army, the Storm Troops, shot, beaten to death or systematically tortured in concentration camps. **Hitler's aim was so to terrorise the German people that no one would dare to resist him by deed or word.**

In spite of these bestial cruelties some Germans were brave enough to carry on the struggle against Hitler, but their power was small and most were killed, beaten into acquiescence, or forced to leave the country.

Meanwhile the army was rapidly growing; in 1935 conscription was reintroduced; the industrialists began to make great profits out of re-armament; the Junkers had their privileges confirmed, and the Nazis enriched themselves by plunder and confiscation.

Political Smash and Grab. When Hitler had established his power in Germany he began to carry out his plan for conquering other nations. **It was a plan which appealed to the Germans.** In March, 1938, German troops occupied Austria. In September, 1938, at Munich, the British and French Prime Ministers, who knew their countries were quite unprepared for war, reluctantly agreed to the Nazi annexation of important border areas of Czechoslovakia, where many of the people were of German speech. In March, 1939, the rest of Czechoslovakia was occupied—a flagrant breach of Hitler's promise to Mr. Chamberlain only six months before.

It was now obvious to everyone that Hitler's dreams of conquest knew no bounds. His next victim was to be Poland. Prussia had held parts of Poland for a hundred and fifty years until, in 1918, the Poles at last won back their freedom. Now Hitler resolved to enslave them again. The British and French Governments solemnly warned him that an attack on Poland would bring both countries into the war.

Hitler, drunk with easy successes, did not believe that we would fight. He thought we were too "decadent." On 1st September, 1939, he seized the Free City of Danzig, his armies entered Poland and the Second World War had begun.

—WHAT THE NAZIS HAVE DONE TO GERMANY—

WHEN Germany is defeated, Hitler and his gang of Nazi leaders will be swept away but it will not be possible to make a clean sweep of the millions of Germans who have at some time worn the Nazi badge. The system will leave a deep mark on German life, and if you are to understand the Germans you must know something of how it worked.

Germany under the Nazis is a "totalitarian state." Hitler is the Dictator, or "Führer" (Leader). He not only doubles the parts of president and chancellor; he is supreme law-giver, supreme judge, head of the civil service, commander-in-chief of the armed forces and leader of the Nazi Party. The Cabinet is there merely to advise him; the parliament (Reichstag) is there merely to hear his decisions and applaud. His position is more despotic than that of King John in England, before Magna Carta limited his powers more than 700 years ago.

At the head of each of the 15 States into which Germany is divided is one of Hitler's yes-men. These state governors (Reichs-Statthalter) appoint the provincial officials; they, on their part, appoint their subordinates and so on down to the smallest employee. No one can be a state or municipal servant in Nazi Germany unless

Hitler and Hitler's yes-men are convinced of his loyalty to themselves.

But that is only half the story.

The Nazi Party. Side by side and interlocking with the Nazi Government is the Nazi Party. The Party has its own network of officials from the Gauleiter, who controls one of the 42 gaus into which Germany is divided for purposes of Party organisation, down to the Blockwart with the modest job of ruling a block of flats.

Although the same man is often both a government official and a Party official, the functions of the government and the Party are theoretically distinct.

The Party's main concern is to keep the people's faith and enthusiasm for Hitler at boiling point and to turn on the heat for any who are still luke-warm. The function of the government is to carry out Hitler's decrees in practice and run the country on the lines he has laid down.

The national army is, of course, in the service of the government, but the Party has a private army for its own purposes. This Party-army is called the **S.A. (Sturm-Abteilungen = Storm Troops)**. But in 1934 there was friction between the S.A. and the regular army and Hitler, who wanted to win the regular army's support, massacred many of the leading S.A. men (including their commander, Captain Röhm).

Hitler's body-guard, **the S.S. (Schutz-Staffel = Black Guards)**, a more carefully selected and better drilled body of thugs, then took the place of the S.A. as Hitler's personal armed force on the home front.

The notorious **Gestapo (Geheime Staats-Polizei = Secret State Police)**, which is responsible for hunting down opponents and killing them or breaking their spirit in concentration camps, is also one of the pillars of Hitler's strength.

All other political parties, and also trade unions, co-operative societies, even boy scout troops and religious organisations for children and young people, were abolished or taken over by the Nazi Party so that no German, man, woman or child, could escape their influence.

When you reach Germany, this evil system will be swept away, but the German people will find it hard to get rid of much of the Nazi creed.

"Mein Kampf." Hitler's crude and violent beliefs, few of them original in German thought, are laid down in his book, *Mein Kampf* (My Struggle), which all Germans are supposed to have read.

According to Hitler the State is something above the people. The individual must give up his rights, his liberties, his beliefs, even his religion, for what is held to be the good of the State. But Hitler claims that the Germans are a very special people; they are not only Aryans (by which he apparently meant natives of Northern Europe); they are also the Master Race, and their destiny is to rule and lead all other nations.

The natural enemies of the Master Race are Non-Aryans (Jews), Bolsheviks and Plutocrats. By "Plutocrats" the Nazis generally mean ourselves and the Americans.

Since it is obviously impossible for a Master Race to have been beaten in battle, the Nazis teach that the German armies were not defeated in 1918; Germany would have won, they say, if the Jews, Bolsheviks and other "traitors" inside the country had not "stabbed her in the back."

The Christian virtues of kindness and justice are thought to be unworthy of the Master Race, and the Nazis have tried to uproot them. This involved Hitler in a conflict with the churches. He not only tried to suppress the Protestants and Catholics, but also encouraged the Nazis to invent semi-pagan religions of their own.

It seems strange that such wild ideas could impose on a European nation in the 20th century, but **woven into Hitler's doctrine are many deep-seated German "complexes," such as hatred of the Jews, a desire to domineer over others** and a readiness to believe that they themselves are being persecuted.

Who, you may ask, are these Nazis, who go in for such perverted ideas and cruel practices?

In the early days, there were some misled idealists among them, but the leaders are wicked and ambitious men, who have used their power to enrich themselves by plundering first their fellow Germans and then other nations. In this way they have become fabulously wealthy. They stand outside and above German law; they have been answerable for their crimes to no one but Hitler, and he encouraged them.

—WHAT THE WAR HAS DONE TO GERMANY—

THE Germany you will see is a very different place from the peace-time Germany.

If you come in from the west you will enter the most-bombed area in Europe. Here the destruction is many times greater than anything you have seen in London, Coventry or Bristol. Compare these figures: in eleven months (September, 1940, to July, 1941) the Germans dropped 7,500 tons of bombs on London—we dropped nearly 10,000 tons on Duisburg in two attacks between Saturday morning and Sunday morning, the 14th to 15th October, 1944. In western towns from Hamburg south through the industrial Ruhr and Rhineland—with Essen, Düsseldorf, Duisburg and many other centers—and east to Nuremberg and Munich, you will see areas that consist largely of heaps of rubble and roofless, windowless shells. Cities like Berlin and Hanover in Central Germany will be no better off.

In all these places communal life has been broken up. Mass evacuations have been carried out, not only of children, but of the grown-up population. Only those remained who were needed to staff such factories as could still operate, and to run the civil defence, salvage, police and other essential services. As fast as repairs were made, the R.A.F. blasted them and added to the earlier destruction.

Tens of thousands of Germans have been killed or injured in these raids, hundreds of thousands have lost their belongings and could not replace them because of the shortage of goods.

The Biter Bit. In Western and Central Germany you will find a war area of bleak poverty and devastation. The Germans have been well and truly paid for what they did to Warsaw, Rotterdam and Belgrade.

But the German people have had other things to bear. Probably more than three and a half million German soldiers have been killed in action and another million severely wounded.

The supply of food for German civilians was restricted even before war began so that they could have "guns instead of butter." During the war their rations have been a good deal lower than ours; they have had much less meat, bread and milk and the quality of the food was inferior.

Many of the people you will see in the towns may be under-nourished, though not starving like the people of Poland and Greece.

On top of all this the German workers who remained in industry; and the millions of women who were drafted into the factories, have been worn out by long hours of hard work, which often followed sleepless nights in air-raid shelters. You must therefore expect to find a population that is hungry, exhausted and on the verge of despair.

You will probably find that public services and supplies are working very imperfectly, and it will be urgently necessary to get them going again. Apart from the partial breakdown due to bombing and defeat, the collapse of the Nazi Party will mean that a good deal of routine work is left undone, for in addition to their main task of regimenting their fellow-Germans, the local Nazi officials have done many useful jobs of organisation and relief.

To complete the picture, you are likely to find bands of **foreign workers** trying to make their way home, mostly men and women **who were carried off to Germany and forced to work there as slaves of the German war-machine**. By the end of the war there will be millions of these foreign workers—Russians, French, Poles, Czechs, Belgians, Italians and others—working in Germany. Prisoners of war, of whom Germany has several millions, will also have to be collected from camps, farms and factories and sent back to their homes.

—WHAT THE GERMANS ARE LIKE—

WHEN you meet the Germans you will probably think they are very much like us.

They look like us, except that there are fewer of the wiry type and more big, fleshy, fair-haired men and women, especially in the north.

But they are not really so much like us as they look.

The Germans have, of course, many good qualities. They are very hard working and thorough; they are obedient and have a great love of tidiness and order. They are keen on education of a formal sort, and are proud of their "culture" and their appreciation of music, art and literature.

But for centuries they have been trained to submit to authority—not because they thought their rulers wise and right, but because obedience was imposed on them by force.

The old Prussian army—and the Nazi army too—set out intentionally to break the spirit of recruits. They were made to do stupid and humiliating things in order to destroy their self respect and turn them into unquestioning fighting machines. This method produced a formidable military force, but it did not produce good human beings. It made the Germans cringe before authority.

GERMANY
BEFORE MARCH, 1938

Railways
Canals

That is one reason why they accepted Hitler. He ordered them about, and most of them liked it. It saved them the trouble of thinking. All they had to do was obey and leave the thinking to him.

It also saved them, they thought, from responsibility. The vile cruelties of the Gestapo and S.S. were nothing to do with them. They did not order them; they did not even want to know about them. The rape of Norway, Holland and Belgium was not their business. It was the business of Hitler and the General Staff.

That is the tale that will be told over and over again by the Germans. They will protest with deep sincerity that they are as innocent as a babe in arms.

But the German people cannot slide out of their responsibility quite so easily. You must remember that Hitler became Chancellor in a strictly legal way. Nearly half the German electors voted for him in the last (comparatively) free election of 1933. With the votes of his Nationalist allies he had a clear majority. The Germans knew what he stood for—it was in his book—and they approved it. Hitler was immensely popular with the majority of Germans: they regarded him as the restorer of German greatness. They welcomed the abolition of unemployment although they knew that it arose from conscription and rearmament. **After the fall of France most Germans supported his**

military conquests with enthusiasm. It was only when they felt the cold wind of defeat that they discovered their consciences.

The Mind of the German. The Germans adore military show. In Nazi Germany everyone has a uniform. If it isn't the uniform of the Army, Navy or Air Force, it is that of the S.A., S.S. or some other Party organisation. Even the little boys and girls have been strutting about in the uniform of the Hitler Youth or the Union of German Girls.

Such uniforms may still impress the Germans, but they will not impress you. But you must do justice to the position of the ordinary German policeman. He will have no authority over British troops, but you should do nothing to make more difficult any task he may be allotted by the Allies.

The uniforms you will respect are those of the British and Allied forces.

It is important that you should **be smart and soldierly** in appearance and behaviour. The Germans think nothing of a slovenly soldier.

You will run across Germans who are genuinely ashamed of being Germans. Even before Hitler made Germany universally hated, they had a sense of national inferiority. They felt that other nations, like the

British, Americans and French, were somehow ahead of them. There is little doubt that Hitler realised this, and used his theory of the Master Race to overcome it. He tried to make the Germans think well of themselves, and he overdid it. There will be some—especially the young ones—who have swallowed the tale that they are members of the Master Race, and are therefore our superiors.

There is no need to say much more about German brutality; it has been unmistakably revealed in the Nazi methods of governing and of waging war. But you may think it strange that the Germans are at the same time sentimental. They love melancholy songs; they easily get sorry for themselves; even childless old couples insist on having their Christmas tree. German soldiers would play with Polish or Russian children, and yet there are enough authentic reports of these same children being shot or burnt or starved to death.

This mixture of sentimentality and callousness does not show a well-balanced mind. The Germans are not good at controlling their feelings. They have a streak of hysteria. You will find that Germans may often fly into a passion if some little thing goes wrong.

How Hitler moulded them. Hitler set to work, for his own purposes, to cultivate these weaknesses and vices of the German character.

He wanted his Nazis to be still more brutal because he thought that in this way he could terrify the German nation, and other nations too, into submission. Tens of thousands of young men in the S.S. have been systematically trained as torturers and executioners. Some went mad in the process, but others reached a point where they can commit any atrocity with indifference or even with pleasure.

Ordinary members of the public have been taught to spy on each other. Little boys and girls in the Hitler Youth have been encouraged to denounce their parents and teachers if they let slip some incautious criticism of Hitler or his government. The result is that no one in Nazi Germany can trust his fellows, friendship and family affection have been undermined, and thousands of anti-Nazi Germans have been forced to pretend—even in their own homes—that they admire the men and principles which in their hearts they despise. Lying and hypocrisy became a necessity.

Hitler's own breaches of faith—especially in his dealings with other nations—were represented as skilful diplomacy. The Germans admired his success and came to admire his methods.

Worst of all, perhaps, it has been drummed into German children in the schools and Hitler Youth that might is right, war the finest form of human activity and Christianity just slushy sentiment. By cramming children's minds with Nazi ideas and preventing any other ideas from reaching them, Hitler hoped to breed a race of robots after his own heart. We cannot yet judge to what extent this inhuman plan has succeeded.

So you will not be surprised if the German proves to be less like us than he appears at first sight.

This does not mean that all Germans are liars, hypocrites and brutes. Even Nazi methods of education have not been so successful as all that; but it does mean that the national character of the Germans has worsened a good deal under Nazi influence. **Be on your Guard.** When you deal with Germans you must be on your guard. **We were taken in by them after the last war**: many of us swallowed their story about the "cruel" Treaty of Versailles, although it was really far more lenient than the terms they themselves had imposed on Russia only a year before; many of us believed their talk about disarmament and the sincerity of their desire for peace. And so we let ourselves in for this war, which has been a good deal bigger than the last. **There are signs that the German leaders are already making plans**

for a Third World War. That must be prevented at all costs.

When you get to Germany it is possible that some civilians will welcome your arrival, and may even look on you as their liberators from Hitler's tyranny. These will be among the Germans who consistently opposed Hitler during his years of success. Not that they made speeches against him or committed sabotage: any who did that are unlikely to be alive to welcome you. But there are many who kept their own counsel and passively opposed Hitler all along.

As a rule they are loyal members of the political parties suppressed by Hitler, mostly workers, but often honest people of the middle classes. Or they are Catholics or Protestants, who have opposed Hitler because of his persecution of Christianity.

But many Germans will pretend they have been anti-Nazis simply because they want to be on the winning side. Among them will be many doubtful characters. Even those who seem to have the best intentions cannot be regarded as trustworthy; they are almost certain to have some axe to grind. That is one of the reasons why you have been instructed not to fraternise with the Germans.

There are fanatical young Nazis—girls as well as boys—whose heads and hearts are still full of the vicious teachings they absorbed in the Hitler Youth. Their talk, if you ever heard it, might sound plausible and even rather fine, for Hitler's propagandists have naturally dressed up his ideas to make them attractive to the young. But remember that the real meaning of Nazism is shown in its vile practices, not in its fair words.

And, quite possibly, you will some day run into one of the genuine thugs, one of the former killers or crooked Nazi bosses. He may try to throw his weight about, or he may cringe and try to curry favour. Such people really respect nothing but force.

The authorities will know how to deal with them.

IF we leave the extreme Nazi ideas out of account, the basic German view of the British is something like this:

The British do not work so hard as the Germans or take their work so seriously.

The British do not organise as well as the Germans. (In fact the German tends to over-organise; this war has shown that our organisation, when we really get down to it, is just as thorough and more flexible.)

But on the whole the Germans admire the British. The efforts of the German Propaganda Ministry to stir up hatred against us have not been, in spite of the R.A.F. raids, a great success. It is probable that of all the occupying troops of the United Nations we and the Americans will be the least unwelcome.

Even Hitler had a grudging respect for us, as he admitted in *Mein Kampf*. He envied us the British Empire and admired the national qualities that went to building it up—imagination, enterprise and tough endurance. He thought we had grown decadent and lost them. Our fighting forces—and the civilians at home—have proved the contrary.

Germans believe we have other national virtues. They think that we are fair, decent and tolerant and and that we have political common sense.

Now that the Nazi dream of world-conquest has been shattered, these homely qualities look all the more attractive, and many Germans would probably say to-day that their ideal of the new Germany is something like Britain.

While you are serving in Germany you are representatives of Britain. Your behaviour will decide their opinion of us.

It is not that we value their opinion for its own sake. It is good for the Germans, however, to see that soldiers of the British democracy are self-controlled and self-respecting, that in dealing with a conquered nation they can be firm, fair and decent. The Germans will have to become fair and decent themselves, if we are to live with them in peace later on.

But the Germans have another pet idea. They claim that we are nationally akin to them, they call us their "cousins." This is part of their theory of the superiority of the Northern races.

The likeness, if it exists at all, is only skin-deep. **The deeper you dig into the German character, the more you realise how different they are from us. So don't be taken in by first impressions.**

The Germans think of the Americans much in the same way as they think of us, but they do not know them so well and many of their ideas come from Hollywood films, which were once very popular in Germany. That is why they think, for instance, that all Americans are rich. Their first idea of the American troops as "amateur" soldiers has been completely disproved by battle experience.

The Germans' attitude to the Russians is quite different. Under Hitler they have been taught to regard the Russians as sub-human. The purpose of this was to remove any scruples they might have had about the barbarous methods of German warfare on the Russian front. The Soviet citizen, Hitler said, was less than a human being, so no treatment could be too cruel for him. The "Bolsheviks" were bracketed with the Jews as Enemy of Mankind No. 1.

When the Red Army began to advance Hitler redoubled this propaganda. He hoped to frighten his troops and the civilians at home into resistance to the death. And to some extent he succeeded.

The severity of the Red Army's fight for liberation is easy to understand. **Hitler, running true to form, attacked Russia while the pact of friendship he had made with her was still in force**; he has spurred on his soldiers and S.S. to commit atrocities more barbarous than anything in modern history—except their own record in Poland.

Ever since the Germans invaded Russia in 1941, their propaganda has been spreading baseless scares about the

"Bolshevik menace." The aim was perfectly clear—it was to drive a wedge between us and our Russian ally. Remember this if the Germans try to spread stories against the Red Army.

—HOW THE GERMANS LIVE—

THE instructions you will receive in Germany will keep you very much apart from the Germans. Probably you will rarely, if ever, enter a house where Germans are living, and neither will you be meeting Germans on social occasions; but you should know something of how they live so as to understand what is going on around you.

Life in any country of Central or Western Europe is not—under peace-time conditions—very different from what it is at home, but there are quite a lot of smaller differences. For instance there is—

Food. Probably you will seldom come across food cooked in the German way. Even if you do, it may be very different from pre-war German food. It is likely to be a long time before German supplies get back to normal.

At its best, German cooking produces some characteristic and appetising dishes. The chief difference from English cooking is in the treatment of vegetables. In place of the English boiled greens the Germans serve a white pickled cabbage called Sauerkohl (sour cabbage) or a red cabbage called Rotkohl. Both are very tasty if you eat them with Wiener Schnitzel (fried veal) or Schweine-kotelett (fried pork cutlet).

The Germans prefer pork and veal to beef and mutton, and cook them better. But the staple meat dish is the sausage. The best German sausage is eaten cold and there are hundreds of varieties of it. Two excellent kinds of sausage are Mettwurst (Wurst = sausage) and Leberwurst (liver sausage).

The Germans are very fond of Torten (pastries), with Schlagsahne (whipped cream), but it will be some time before such luxuries are obtainable again at the Konditorei (confectioner's). The Germans don't know how to make tea, but they are quite expert with coffee. However, for the present their coffee is "ersatz."

"Beer is best." The favourite German drink is beer. Under war conditions it has been diluted much more even than English beer, but normally it is regarded as the pleasantest beer in Europe. There are hundreds of brews; two of the most famous are Münchener (from Munich) and Pilsener (from Pilsen in Czechoslovakia). Local beers are either light (hell) or dark (dunkel). All German beers are iced.

Western Germany produces some of the choicest wine on the Continent, such as Moselle wine and Rhine wine (which we call "hock"). Compared with prices in Britain wine is cheap.

Whiskey and gin will be scarce and of poor quality (unless imported from Britain), **but there are many kinds of spirits called schnaps. The cheaper sorts are guaranteed to take the skin off one's throat.**

Entertainment. Entertainment will be provided for you by E.N.S.A. in your own camp or barracks and most German places of entertainment will be out of bounds. The Germans, of course, will be going to cinemas where it is probable that British, American and Russian films will be shown. There may also be German films—non-political ones. But German films, which were very good before 1933, suffered like so many other things because Hitler insisted on making them an instrument of Nazi propaganda, and there may at first be very few available which are free from this taint. This is also true of German plays.

Sport. The Germans have only taken to sport during the last thirty years, but they are keen and capable performers. They learnt most of their sport from us. Football is the most popular game, but is played less vigorously than in Britain; charging is regarded as rough play. Football is entirely amateur, and "pools" are unknown. There is no cricket, but plenty of athletics, some tennis and a little golf. Boxing and wrestling are both popular spectacles, and the Germans go in for a good deal of cycle racing.

Health. The standards of health, normally high, have fallen as a result of the war. Venereal diseases are prevalent. **A German expert stated (May, 1943), "Venereal diseases strike at every fourth person between the ages of 15 and 41."**

Women. Before Hitler came to power the German woman was winning the same freedom to live her own life as British women enjoy, but the Nazis took away her newly won rights and made her again the traditional Hausfrau (housewife). Shortage of man-power in war time brought German women back into the professions, but only on sufferance.

Under the shock of defeat standards of personal honour, already undermined by the Nazis, will sink still lower. Numbers of German women will be willing, if they can get the chance, to make themselves cheap for what they can get out of you. After the last war prostitutes streamed into the zone occupied by British and American troops. They will probably try this again, even though this time you will be living apart from the Germans. Be on your guard. Most of them will be infected.

Marriages between members of British forces and Germans are, as you know, forbidden.

But for this prohibition such marriages would certainly take place. Germany will not be a pleasant place to live in for some time after the war, and German girls know that, if they marry British husbands, they will become British with all the advantages of belonging to a victor nation instead of to a vanquished one. Many German girls will be just waiting for the chance to marry a Briton—whether they care for him or not. When once they had their marriage lines he would have served his purpose.

During the last occupation there were a number of marriages between British soldiers and German girls. The great majority of these marriages soon came to grief. When the couples returned to England they found themselves lonely and friendless, and this resulted only in unhappiness for the wife, the husband and the children. That is one reason—though not the only one—why this time they will not be allowed.

Religion. Large parts of Germany have been Protestant since the Reformation in the early 16th century, when Martin Luther led the revolt against the papacy. To-day about two-thirds of Germany is Protestant and one-third Catholic; the Protestants are strongest in North and Central Germany, the Catholics in the west, south and south-east.

Many of the Catholic churches are of great beauty and antiquity. Some, like Cologne Cathedral, have unfortunately suffered in raids, but there are many other noble and ancient churches which are well worth seeing. A few of the most famous are: in Central Germany, the cathedrals of Naumburg and Hildesheim; in South Germany those of Speyer, Bamberg and Worms.

Music. The Germans are extremely fond of music and have produced composers and performers of great eminence. Beethoven, Bach, Brahms, Wagner were all Germans. There are fine concerts of classical music in most of the larger German towns.

Jazz and Swing are frowned on by the Nazis because they are not considered Nordic, but the Germans are fond of dancing, and some dance bands are still playing the latest American and British hits.

Literature. Many of the best German writers had opposed Hitler before his advent to power or had expressed a view of life contrary to Fascism. Their books were therefore banned in Germany and copies of many of them publicly burnt. Jewish writers, some of whom had been in the front rank, were also banned. It has been difficult for a writer to earn a living in Germany unless he was willing to use his talents to spread Nazi ideas. So if you know German and wish to read German books you will find few that are not tainted by Hitler-propaganda, unless they were written by anti-Nazi refugees and published, abroad.

For the same reasons, modern painters and scientists of independent thought have been silenced or forced to escape from the great intellectual prison of Hitler-Germany.

It will take a long time for Germany to reach again the high level she had attained in the things of the mind under the free republic that preceded Hitler.

General. The rule of the road is: Keep to the **Right— not** to the **Left** as in Britain.

In Germany every town and village has a mayor (*Bürgermeister*); if it is a town with a population of over 20,000 he is probably called an *Oberbürgermeister*. But whatever his title, he has essential administrative duties to perform and is a more important official than his opposite number in England.

If you have to give orders to German civilians, give them in a firm, military manner. The German civilian is used to it and expects it.

The Germans are very short of clothes and footwear. Look out for attempts to steal, beg or buy your boots, shirts and underclothes. You don't need to be told that it is a serious offence to sell or give away Government property.

If you should be billeted in a German household—though this will very seldom happen—be courteous but aloof, avoid loose talk and loose conduct, and keep your eyes and ears open.

With their habitual reverence for all things military, the Germans will be quick to notice any slackness in the dress or bearing of British troops. Don't let your Country or your Unit down.

It is only natural that Germans who have suffered personally under Nazi oppression will try to take revenge on their local tyrants. They will regard this as their own affair and will resent interference. Don't go looking for trouble.

The Nazis have had great experience in organising incidents to cause trouble or to influence public opinion. The die-hards (mostly young products of the Hitler Youth) may try to play similar tricks even when their country has been occupied. **If the incident is small, keep your head and refuse to be impressed or put out of countenance. If it is big, the Allied authorities will deal with it.**

As soon as the pressure of Hitlerism is removed, political parties will spring up again. Even if they have names similar to our parties they will have different problems and different aims. **Steer clear of anything connected with German politics.**

—MONEY—

THE smallest German coin is the Pfennig. 100 Pfennigs make one Mark or more formally "Reichsmark."

When you enter Germany you will be given official information about the number of Marks which go to the £.

German coins at present in circulation are:—

1, 5, and 10 Pfennig pieces, made of zinc, 5 and 10 Pfennig pieces made of an aluminium-bronze alloy, an aluminium 50 Pfennig piece, and 2 Mark and 5 Mark pieces of a silver-copper alloy.

In addition to these coins you may come across the following notes: 1, 2 and 5 Mark notes issued by the Rentenbank, and 10, 20, 50, 100 and 1,000 Mark notes issued by the Reichsbank

Wherever you are stationed in Germany you will find at first that there is practically nothing to buy. Food, clothing and tobacco will be severely rationed; there will be no little things you can send home as gifts; the shops will be empty. **Your needs will be looked after by Navy, Army and R.A.F. issue and the NAAFI stores.** The only thing you can buy from the Germans will be a glass of beer or wine.

It will be a long time before the basic needs of the German population are satisfied and inessential goods are again produced.

So for the time being there is little you can do with your pay except save it. You should therefore draw the minimum.

ENGLISH is taught in all German secondary schools and is a compulsory subject in most; it is also taught in large numbers of commercial and language schools throughout the country, so that many Germans have at least a smattering of English. In any hotel or larger restaurant, or government or municipal office; or large shop, there will almost certainly be someone who speaks English.

But in the depths of the country or in working-class districts, you may have to speak German if you cannot get through with the language of signs.

Many German words are similar to English, especially those in most common use. For instance, Mann = man, Haus = house, Garten = garden, Butter = butter, and Brot=bread. This is because the two languages have grown largely from the same root.

A list of words and phrases is printed at the end of this book, and indications are given of how to pronounce them.

The pronunciation is straightforward except for two or three German sounds which we do not use in English.

The golden rule in trying to speak a language you do not know is to be as simple as possible. Take a two-year-old child as your model. Don't try to make sentences; use nouns and verbs.

At the beginning try to ask questions which can be answered by Ja (yes) or Nein (no). Speak in a normal voice; you will not make your meaning any clearer by shouting.

If you are not understood, point to the word or sentence in your list of phrases.

—DO'S—

REMEMBER you are a representative of the British Commonwealth.

KEEP your eyes and ears open.

BE SMART and soldierly in dress and bearing.

AVOID loose talk and loose conduct.

BE FIRM AND FAIR in any dealings with Germans.

KEEP GERMANS AT A DISTANCE, even those with whom you have official dealings.

STEER CLEAR of all disputes between German political parties.

GO EASY on Schnaps.

REMEMBER that in Germany "venereal diseases strike at every fourth person between the ages of 15 and 41."

—DON'TS—

DON'T sell or give away dress or equipment.

DON'T be sentimental. If things are tough for the Germans they have only themselves to blame. They made things much worse for the innocent people of the countries they occupied.

DON'T believe German accounts of the war or the events that led up to it. The Germans got their ideas on these subjects from lying propaganda.

DON'T fall for political hard-luck stories.

DON'T believe tales against our Allies or the Dominions. They are aimed at sowing ill will between us.

DON'T be taken in by surface resemblances between the Germans and ourselves.

DON'T go looking for trouble.

—WORDS AND PHRASES—

Orders

Hands up!	Hände hoch! **hend**a hohk
Open your hands!	Öffnen Sie die Hände! **uff**nen zee dee **hend**a
Halt! Who goes there?	Halt! Wer da? *hahlt vair dah*
Give me your papers	Geben Sie mir Ihre Papiere **gay**ben zee meer eera pa**peer**a
Sit down!	Setzen Sie sich! **zet**zen zee zish
Stand up!	Stehen Sie auf **shtay**en zee owf

General

Good morning (day, evening)	Guten Morgen (Tag, Abend) **goo**ten **mor**gen (tahk, **ah**bent)
Excuse me	Entschuldigen Sie *ents**shoold**iggen zee*
I beg your pardon	Verzeihung *fair**tsy**oong*
Is there anyone who speaks English?	Spricht jemand englisch? *shprisht **yay**mant **eng**lish*
Please write (read) this	Bitte schreiben Sie (lesen Sie) das **Bitt**a **shry**ben zee (**lay**zen zee) dass
Who are you?	Wer sind Sie? *vair zint zee*
What is your name?	Wie heissen Sie? *vee **hy**ssen zee*

53

Where do you live?	Wo wohnen Sie? *vo* **vohn**en *zee*
Come in!	Herein! *hair***ine**!
Quick, slowly	Schnell, langsam *shnell,* **lank***sahm*
It is late (early)	Es ist spät (früh) *es ist shpate (free)*
I am in a hurry	Ich habe es eilig *ish* **hah***ba es* **eye***lish*
Take care!	Achtung! or Vorsicht! **ahk***toong!* **fore***zisht!*
Wait here, please	Warten Sie hier, bitte **vahr***ten zee here* **bitta**
We are friends	Wir sind Freunde *veer zint* **froyn***da*
Don't be afraid	Keine Angst **ky***na angst*
I will return later	Ich komme später zurück *ish* **komm***a* **shpat***er tsoo***rick**
I will meet you here at . . . o'clock	Ich treffe Sie hier um . . . Uhr *ish* **treff***a zee here oom . . . oor*
What do you call this?	Wie heisst dies? *vee* **hy***st dees?*
What does that mean?	Was bedeutet das? *vahss be***doyt***et dass?*
Say it again	Wiederholen Sie es *veeder***hohl***en zee ess*
I don't understand	Ich verstehe nicht *ish fair***shtay***a nisht*
Do you understand?	Verstehen Sie? *fair***shtay***en zee?*

Please speak slowly (write it down)	Bitte sprechen Sie langsam **bitt**a **shpresh**en zee **lank**sahm (schreiben Sie es auf) (**shry**ben zee ess owf)
What do you want?	Was wollen Sie? vahss **voll**en zee?
What is the matter?	Was ist los? vahss ist lohs?
What is the time?	Wie spät ist es? vee shpate ist ess?
Where are you going?	Wo gehen sie hin? vo **gay**en zee hin?
What nationality are you?	Was für ein Landsmann sind Sie? vahss feer ine **lants**mahn zint zee?
Are you German (French)?	Sind Sie Deutscher (Franzose)? zint zee **doy**cher (frahn**tsoh**za)?
What is the name of this town (this village)?	Wie heisst diese Stadt (dieses Dorf)? vee hyst **dee**za shtat (**dee**zes dorf)?
Have you seen any soldiers?	Haben Sie Soldaten gesehen? **hah**ben zee zol**dah**ten ge**zayn**?
What kind of soldiers?	Was für Soldaten? vahss feer zol**dah**ten?
Go away, please	Bitte gehen Sie weg **bitt**a **gay**en zee veck
I cannot talk to you now	Ich kann jetzt nicht mit Ihnen sprechen ish khan yetst misht mit **een**en **shpresh**en
I know nothing about it	Ich weiss nichts davon ish vice nishts da**fon**

Travelling by Road

Which is the way to —?	Wie kommt man nach —? vee kommt mahn nahk —?

How far is it to —?	Wie weit ist es nach —? *vee vite ist ess nahk —?*
Where does this road lead to?	Wohin führt diese Strasse? *vohin feert deeza shtrahssa?*
Where am I now? Show me on this map	Wo bin ich jetzt? Zeigen Sie es *vo bin ish yetzt? tsygen zee ess* mir auf diesem Plan *meer owf deezem plahn*
I have lost my way	Ich habe den Weg verloren *ish hahba dain vaik fairlohren*
Stop! Go back!	Stopp! Zurück! *shtop! tsoorick!*
Go on!	Weiterfahren! *vyter-fahren!*
Danger!	Achtung, Gefahr! *ahktoong, gefahr!*
Main road, good road, secondary road, track	Chaussee, gute Strasse, *shosay goota shtrahssa,* Nebenstrasse, Fahrweg *nayben-shtrahssa, fahrvaik*
Road closed. No thoroughfare	Gesperrt. Kein Durchgang *geshpalvt. kine doorshgang*
One-way street (traffic)	Einbahnstrasse (-verkehr) *inebahn-shtrahssa (-fairkair)*
Keep to the left (right)	Links (rechts) fahren *links (reshts) fahren*
Bicycle, horse, mule, cart	Fahrrad, Pferd, Maultier, Wagen *fahr-raht, pfairt, mowlteer, Vahgen*

Car Repairs

My car (lorry) has broken down	Mein Wagen (Lastwagen) hat *mine vahgen (lastvahgen) haht* eine Panne gehabt *eyena panna gehahbt*

Where is the nearest garage?	Wo ist die nächste Garage? *vo ist dee* **naiksta** *ga***rah***ja?*
Can you repair (replace) this?	Können Sie das reparieren (auswechseln)? **kenn***en zee dass reppa***reeren** **(owssvexeln***)?*
Can you fetch (tow) my car?	Können Sie meinen Wagen **kenn***en zee* **my***nen* **vah***gen* holen (abschleppen)? **hoh***len* **(ap-shlepp***en)?*
I need petrol (oil, water)	Ich brauche Benzin (Oel, Wasser) *ish* **brow***ka bent***seen** *(ull, vahss***er)**
Can you lend me some tools?	Können Sie mir Werkzeuge leihen? **kenn***en zee meer* **vairk***tsoyga* **ly***en?*

Travelling by Rail

Where is the railway station?	Wo ist der Bahnhof? *vo ist dair* **bahn***hof?*
When is there a train to —?	Wann fährt ein Zug nach —? *vahn fairt ine tsook nahk —?*
What time does it arrive?	Wann kommt er an? *vahn kommt air an?*
Do I have to change?	Muss ich umsteigen? *mooss ish* **oom***shtygen?*
A single (return) ticket to —	Eine Fahrkarte (Rückfahrkarte) nach — **eye***na* **fahr***karta* **(rick***fahrkarta) nahk —*
Ticket office	Fahrkartenausgabe **fahr***karten-***owss***gahba*
Refreshment room	Bahnhofrestaurant **bahn***hof-resto***rong**

The Country, the Sea

Bridge, ford, river	Brücke, Furt, Fluss **brick**a, *foort, flooss*
Mountain, forest, wood, canal	Berg, Forst, Wald, Kanal *bairg, forst, vahlt, kan***ahl**
Farm	Bauernhof **bow**ern-hof
Are the trees in that wood thick?	Stehen die Bäume dicht in diesem Wald? **shtay**en dee **boy**ma disht in **dee**zem vahlt?
Field, ploughed field, pasture	Feld, Acker, Wiese *felt,* **ack**er, **vee**za
Whose cattle (horses) are these?	Wem gehören dieses Vieh (diese Pferde)? *vaim ge***hur**en **dee**zes fee (**dee**za **pfair**da)?
Can we sleep in your barn (out-buildings)?	Können wir in Ihrer Scheune **kenn**en veer **ee**rer **shoy**na (Anbau) schlafen? (**ahn**bow) **shlah**fen?
Fodder, hay, straw, wheat, crops	Futter, Heu, Stroh, Korn, Ernte **foot**er, hoy, shtroh, korrn, **airn**ta
Horse, cow, sheep, goat, chicken goose	Pferd, Kuh, Schaf, Ziege, Huhn, Gans *pfairt, koo, shahf,* **tsee**ga, hoon, gahnss
Is there a spring (well, stream) near here?	Gibt es eine Quelle (einen *geebt ess* **eye**na **kvell**a **eye**nen Brunnen, ein Bach) in der Nähe? **broo**nen, ine bahk) in dair **nay**a?

Accommodation, Baths

Where can I get a bed?	Wo kann ich schlafen? *vo kahn ish* **shlah**fen?
These are my (our) billets	Ich bin (wir sind) hier einquartiert *ish bin (veer zint) here* **ine**-kvarteert

May I (we) come in?	Darf ich (dürfen wir) eintreten? *darf ish (**deer**fen veer) **ine**-trayten?*
I shall be returning late (leaving early)	Ich komme spät zurück (gehe früh fort) *ish **komm**a shpate tsoorick (**gay**a free fort)*
Can we have something to eat (drink)?	Können wir etwas zu essen **kenn**en veer et**vahss** tsoo **ess**en (trinken) bekommen? *(**trink**en) be**komm**en?*
May I have a key?	Kann ich einen Schlüssel haben? *kahn ish **eye**nen **shliss**el **hah**ben?*
Where is the light?	Wo ist das Licht? *vo ist dass lisht?*
A hot bath, soap, towel	Ein warmes Bad, Seife, Handtuch *ine **vahr**mes baht, **zyf**a, **hahn**t-toohk*
Lavatory, cloakroom, dining room	Abort, Garderobe, Esszimmer **ahp**ort, **gar**da-**roh**ba, **ess**tsimmer

Food, Drink

Where can I eat (drink)?	Wo kann ich essen (trinken)? *vo kahn ish **ess**en (**trink**en)?*
May I have breakfast (supper, dinner)	Kann ich Frühstück (Mittagessen, *kahn ish **free**shtick (**mitt**ahk-**ess**en, Abendbrot) haben? **ah**bent-broht) **hah**ben?*
Menu, bottle, cup, glass, jug	Speisekarte, Flasche, Tasse, Glas, Krug **shpy**za-karta, **flash**a, **tahss**a, glahss, krook
Knife, fork, plate, spoon	Messer, Gabel, Teller, Löffel **mess**er, **gah**bel, **tell**er, **leff**el
Bread, butter, cheese, eggs	Brot, Butter, Käse, Eier broht, **boot**er, **kay**za, **ey**er
Fish, meat, vegetables	Fisch, Fleisch, Gemüse *fish, flysh, ge**mee**za*

The butcher (greengrocer)	Der Fleischer (Gemüsehändler) *dair* **fly***sher (ge***mee***za-***hend***ler)*
The fruiterer, apples, pears, plums	Der Obsthändler, Äpfel, Birnen, Pflaumen *dair* **obst***-hendler,* **ep***fel,* **beer***nen,* **Pflow***men*
How much a pound (kilo, liter)?	Was kostet das Pfund, (Kilo, Liter)? *vahss* **kos***tet dass pfoont (***kee***lo,* **lee***ter)?*
Drinking water, milk, tea, coffee	Trinkwasser, Milch, Tee, Kaffee **trink***vahsser, milsh, tay, ka***fay**
Wine, beer, cider	Wein, Bier, Apfelwein *vine, beèr,* **ap***fel-vine*

Entertainment

Theatre, cinema, music-hall	Theater, Kino, Variété *tay***ah***ter,* **keen***o, vareeay***tay**
What time does the show begin?	Wann beginnt die Vorstellung? *vahn be***ginnt** *dee* **fore***shtelloong?*
What price are the seats?	Was kosten die Plätze? *vahss* **kos***ten dee* **plet***za?*
Broadcasting, programme, wireless set	Radio, Programm, Radioempfänger **rah***deeoh, pro***gramm, rah***deeoh-* *emp***feng***er*

Public Notices

Notice, advertisement	Anschlag, Anzeige **ahn***shlahk,* **ahn***tsyga*
It is forbidden	Es ist verboten *ess ist fair***boh***ten*
Smoking (spitting) forbidden	Rauchen (Spucken) verboten **row***ken (***shpook***en) fair***boh***ten*
Entrance free, entrance forbidden	Eintritt frei, Eintritt verboten **ine***tritt fry,* **ine***tritt fair***boh***ten*

Stopping-place (bus, tram)	Haltestelle, Strassenbahn *hahlta-***shtell***a,* **shtrah***ssenbahn*
Bus	Omnibus *omni***booss**
Do not touch, keep off the grass, high tension	Nicht berühren, den Rasen nicht betreten, Hochspannung *nisht be***reer***en, dain* **rah***zen nisht* *be***tray***ten,* **hohk***shpannoong*
Private property	Privateigentum *pree***vaht-***eyegentoom*
Ladies, Gentlemen	Damen, Herren **dah***men,* **hair***en*
Vacant, engaged	Frei, besetzt *fry, be***zetst**
Open, closed	Offen, geschlossen **off***en, ge***shloss***en*

Accidents

Where is the doctor (chemist)?	Wo ist der Arzt (Apotheker)? *vo ist dair artst (appo***tak***er)?*
Fetch a doctor, please	Bitte holen Sie einen Arzt **bitt***a* **hoh***len zee* **eye***nen artst*
Help quickly	Helfen Sie schnell **helf***en zee shnell*
There has been an accident	Ein Unfall ist geschehen *ine* **oon***fall ist ge***shay***en*
I have been wounded (injured)	Ich bin verwundet (verletzt) *ish bin fair***voon***det (fair***letst***)*

—SECURITY NOTE—

If there is no open fighting in the part of Germany in which you find yourself you may think that there is no longer any special need for security.

This is not the case. Germans must still be regarded as dangerous enemies until the final Peace Settlement has been concluded and after the occupation of Germany has ended.

Security is therefore as important as ever. In battle, breaches of security may cost men's lives; under conditions behind the line the danger is not so immediate. Such breaches, will, however, assist those Germans who are working under-ground against us, and, make no mistake about it, there will be plenty of them.

You will have read in this book all about the character of the Germans, and will know what to expect from them, especially from the Nazi elements. Your attention should therefore be firmly and continually fixed on the following points with regard to which the necessity for security remains paramount:—

1. Attempts by propaganda and agents to secure sympathy for the German people and to convince you that they have had a raw deal.

2. Attempts by propaganda and agents to create ill-feeling between us and our Allies, and in particular to stir up anti-Russian feeling.

3. Attempts to sabotage, and to injure the Allied Forces in Germany.

4. Attempts to obtain information as to the movements, dispositions and activities of our Forces, and other information of a military nature, such as advance information of projected operations, search parties, raids and similar intentions.

In order to combat this, you should constantly bear in mind the following:—

Be careful what you say—not only to civilians, but in their hearing. Many more Germans than you think understand and speak English.

Be guarded in what you say on the telephone. Remember that a telephone line is never private.

Remember that propaganda will be used in many forms—some crude and obvious, but much of it subtle and difficult to recognise.

Don't be too ready to listen to stories told by attractive women. They may be acting under orders.

Pay especial attention to security of documents, and don't leave letters and private diaries lying about. Although apparently harmless, they may contain information of value to the enemy.

Report any suspicious characters *at once* to your Unit Security Officer or to a Field Security Officer.

If you have to check identity documents, be scrupulously thorough in assuring yourself that the bearer is all that he claims to be. And finally never leave weapons or ammunition unguarded. Remember the saboteur and the assassin.

Life in Germany will demand your constant vigilance, alertness and self-confidence. Each one of you has a job to do. See that you carry it through, however irksome it may seem, with goodwill and determination. The more thorough we are now the less likely are we to have trouble in the future.